What Is
ASIAN-BLACK
SOLIDARITY?

VIRGINIA LOH-HAGAN

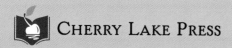
CHERRY LAKE PRESS

Published in the United States of America by Cherry Lake Publishing Group
Ann Arbor, Michigan
www.cherrylakepublishing.com

Reading Adviser: Beth Walker Gambro, MS, Ed., Reading Consultant, Yorkville, IL
Book Design and Cover Art: Felicia Macheske

Photo Credits: © insta_photos/Shutterstock.com, 5; © cheapbooks/Shutterstock.com, 7; Library of Congress, United States. War Relocation Authority, 1942, LOC Control No: 2003689106, 11; © Veja/Shutterstock.com, 12; © Pereslavtseva Katerina/Shutterstock.com, 15; © FeyginFoto/Shutterstock.com, 16; © KiyechkaSo/Shutterstock.com, 19; © Ghawam Kouchaki/Shutterstock.com, 21; © Bykofoto/Shutterstock.com, 22; © Nestor Rizhniak/Shutterstock.com, 25; © Monkey Business Images/Shutterstock.com, 27; © Mike_shots/Shutterstock.com, 29; © vasara/Shutterstock.com, 30

Graphics Throughout: © debra hughes/Shutterstock.com

Cherry Lake Press is an imprint of Cherry Lake Publishing Group.

Library of Congress Cataloging-in-Publication Data

Names: Loh-Hagan, Virginia, author.
Title: What is Asian-Black solidarity? / Virginia Loh-Hagan.
Description: Ann Arbor, Michigan : Cherry Lake Publishing, [2022] | Series:
Racial justice in America: Asian American Pacific Islander | Audience: Grades 4-6 | Summary: "Students will learn about Asian-Black solidarity and discover how the cooperation can help dismantle harmful racism in America. This series explores the issues specific to the AAPI community in a comprehensive, honest, and age-appropriate way. Series is written by Virginia Loh-Hagan, a prolific author, advocate, and director of the San Diego State University Asian Pacific Islander Desi American Resource Center. Developed in conjunction with educator, advocate, and author Kelisa Wing, these books were created to reach children of all races and encourage them to approach race issues with open eyes and minds. Books include 21st Century Skills and content, an activity across books, table of contents, glossary, index, author biography, sidebars, and educational matter"—Provided by publisher.
Identifiers: LCCN 2021047072 | ISBN 9781534199378 (hardcover) | ISBN 9781668900512 (paperback) | ISBN 9781668906279 (ebook) | ISBN 9781668901953 (pdf)
Subjects: LCSH: African Americans—Relations with Asian Americans—Juvenile literature. | Asian Americans—Social conditions—Juvenile literature. | African Americans—Social conditions—Juvenile literature. | United States—Race relations—Juvenile literature.
Classification: LCC E185.615 .L64 2022 | DDC 305.800973—dc23
LC record available at https://lccn.loc.gov/2021047072

Cherry Lake Publishing Group would like to acknowledge the work of the Partnership for 21st Century Learning, a Network of Battelle for Kids. Please visit *http://www.battelleforkids.org/networks/p21* for more information.

Printed in the United States of America

Dr. Virginia Loh-Hagan is an author, former K-8 teacher, curriculum designer, and university professor. She's currently the director of the Asian Pacific Islander Desi American (APIDA) Center at San Diego State University. She identifies as Chinese American and is committed to amplifying APIDA communities. She lives in San Diego with her one very tall husband and two very naughty dogs.

CHAPTER 1

What Is Asian-Black Solidarity?

Asian Americans are a strong community. But like other people of color, they are suffering. They are denied justice. They struggle under White **supremacy**.

In the 1960s, activists first used the term "Asian American." They were inspired by the Black Power movement. They wanted to unite Asian groups. Before this, Asian immigrants were known by their **ethnicities**. For example, they were called "Chinese American" or "Indian American." They acted as separate groups. But they were mistreated as one big group. So they joined forces. As "Asian Americans," they had more power.

Today, they are also called "Asian American Pacific Islander (AAPI)." Another term is "Asian Pacific Islander **Desi** American (APIDA)." These terms are more **inclusive**, meaning that they apply to more Asian people. But they don't fully represent this community. Asian Americans are diverse. They have unique cultures, histories, and languages. It's important to remember this.

Asian Americans are part of the American story. They have made significant contributions and continue to do so. Yet, they are often pushed to the margins. In the 1800s, they immigrated in large numbers. Since then, they have faced discrimination. They have fought to be seen and heard. Their fight for racial justice continues today.

Think about what you have learned in school. How many Asian Americans did you study?

People of color want liberation. They want to be free of injustice. Activists fight to change systems. To achieve liberation, communities of color must be united. They share the common goal of ending White supremacy. Asian Americans and Black Americans have been pitted against each other. This allows White supremacy to win. However, they have also stood in solidarity. They have joined forces to fight against racism.

Both communities have been oppressed. They have been excluded. They have been imprisoned. They have been harmed by hate in many ways. But they have been harmed in different ways. Black Americans have been enslaved. They have been stripped of their human rights. They are the target of much hate. Many of society's systems are set up to punish Black Americans.

Asian-Black solidarity is the key to liberation. Yuri Kochiyama was a Japanese American activist. She was a lifelong champion for Asian-Black solidarity. She said, "Serve the people at the bottom. The people at the top don't need your help." She also said, "We are all part of one another."

This book unpacks Asian-Black solidarity. Learn more so that you can do more.

Think about your friends. Do you have friends from diverse communities?

AMPLIFY AN ACTIVIST!

Activists change our world for the better. Haunani-Kay Trask fought for Hawaiian independence. She fought to preserve Hawaiian culture. In college, she supported the Black Panther Party. She learned a lot from the Black civil rights movement and the American Indian Movement. She said, "Resistance is its own reward."

CHAPTER 2

What Is the History of Asian-Black Solidarity?

There are many examples of Asian-Black solidarity. Working together, these groups have made the world a little more just.

In the 1800s, the United States had many racist laws banning Asians from immigrating. Frederick Douglass was a Black American activist. He spoke in support of Asian immigration.

Early South Asian immigrants came from the Punjab and Bengal areas of India. Moksad Ali was a silk trader. In the late 1800s, he settled in New Orleans, Louisiana. He was rejected by White society. But he was welcomed by the Black community. He married a Black woman. Many multi-racial families had similar stories. Together, they faced anti-Asian exclusion and Jim Crow segregation laws.

These racist laws were in force in southern states until the 1960s.

In 1898, the Philippine islands became a U.S. colony after years of Spanish rule. Filipinos wanted to control their own country. They fought for independence during the Philippine-American War from 1899 to 1902. Many Black American activists supported Philippine independence. Many Black American soldiers joined the Filipino freedom fighters. They didn't like the idea of helping the country that had enslaved them oppress another community of color.

In 1941, Japan attacked Pearl Harbor in Hawaii, causing the United States to enter World War II (1939–1945). President Franklin D. Roosevelt passed a law forcing Japanese Americans into camps. The *California Eagle* was a Black newspaper that strongly criticized Japanese incarceration. Its writers argued that Japanese Americans should reclaim their former homes after being released.

Think about ways people have helped you. What are some ways you have helped others?

Joe Ishikawa was a Japanese American. He was incarcerated at a camp. After being released, he moved to Lincoln, Nebraska. The city had a community pool. Black Americans were the only group not allowed to use it. Ishikawa worked for the city. He quit in protest. He could not support racism against Black Americans. He wrote letters to city leaders. He helped organize a group to overturn the city rule.

The Emergency Detention Act of 1950 was a racist law. It allowed the United States to imprison anyone suspected of being a traitor. In the late 1960s, this law was used to threaten Black American activists. The Japanese American Citizen League (JACL) stepped in. The law was overturned.

During the 1960s, the United States fought in the Vietnam War (1959–1975). Many Black American leaders opposed this war. In 1967, they held a peace march in the Harlem area of New York City. Black activists carried signs that read, "Black men should fight White racism, not Vietnamese freedom fighters."

In 1968, students at San Francisco State University in California formed the Third World Liberation Front (TWLF). Black and Asian American student activists worked with other students of color. They fought to end racist college admission policies. They worked to include more ethnic studies programs.

Think about what Joe Ishikawa did. How did his being incarcerated inspire his activism for Black communities?

LEARN FROM OUR PAST!

Let's not repeat the mistakes of our past. In 1949, Los Angeles city leaders wanted to build a police center in Little Tokyo. This would have evicted more than 2,000 Japanese, Filipino, and Black Americans. Black and Asian American activists fought together for public housing. City laws need to consider the needs of low-income communities.

Many Asian American activists supported the Black Power movement in the 1960s. Yuri Kochiyama was a major leader. She fought for reparations for Japanese incarceration. Reparations are money paid to people who have been wronged. She also fought for reparations for Black Americans, who continue to suffer from the effects of slavery. Grace Lee Boggs was a Chinese American activist who also worked with Black communities, especially in Detroit, Michigan.

Think about a time you hurt someone. How did you make amends for it?

The International Hotel, or I-Hotel, was in San Francisco. It provided low-rent housing to elderly Filipino immigrants. In the 1970s, city leaders violently kicked out the residents. Black American activists stood in solidarity with Asian Americans as they linked arms in protest. They encircled the hotel, trying to keep police from raiding it.

In 1982, Vincent Chin was killed. Chin was a Chinese American man living in Detroit, Michigan. Two White men killed Chin in a bar. They blamed Asians for the decline of the American car industry. Jesse Jackson was a Black American activist. He stood in solidarity with Asian American activists who protested Chin's murder. This helped inspire an Asian American movement for more civil rights.

In 2005, Hurricane Katrina destroyed much of New Orleans, Louisiana. Vietnamese Americans lived in an area of the city called Village de L'Est. City leaders used their community as a dump site. Vietnamese Americans fought against this. They were joined by Black community leaders.

CHAPTER 3

What Does Asian-Black Solidarity Look Like Today?

Asian-Black solidarity continues today. Asians 4 Black Lives is a coalition of Asian Americans. Their mission statement reads, "We support the safety, justice, and resilience of Black communities—so all our communities can prosper. We are not an organization, but we are organized. #BlackLivesMatter."

Trayvon Martin was a Black American teenager. In 2012, he was killed. In 2013, his killer was found not guilty. To many Black Americans, this was yet another example of injustice. To many Asian Americans, this reminded them of Vincent Chin's murder. Chin's killers received no jail time for committing a hate crime.

In response, Black Lives Matter started in 2013. They fight against police brutality and violence against Black people. Asians 4 Black Lives formed soon after to support Black Lives Matter. They have marched and protested. They have organized boycotts, which are protests involving refusing to buy products or participate in something. They have built houses for low-income people. They have fought for more just laws.

Asians 4 Black Lives is also working with Letters for Black Lives. Letters for Black Lives began as a group of Asian Americans and Canadians. They provide resources to deal with anti-Blackness. They encourage discussions between older and younger generations about Black Lives Matter. They provide resources in multiple languages.

Think about Black Lives Matter. How can you support this movement?

Think about what it means to defund the police. How can we keep our communities safe?

STAY ACTIVE ON SOCIAL!

Stay connected on social media. It is a great way to learn more. Follow these hashtags:

- **#Asians4BlackLives** This hashtag represents activists committed to supporting Black communities.

- **#BlackAsianSolidarity** This hashtag shares resources and readings.

- **#Ktown4BlackLives** This hashtag was started by an activist group in Los Angeles's Koreatown. It is focused on working toward collective liberation. It centers Black liberation.

There was much racial unrest in 2020. On February 23, Ahmaud Arbery was shot while jogging. On March 13, Breonna Taylor was shot in her own house. On May 25, George Floyd was killed after a police officer knelt on his neck for 9 minutes. His last words were, "I can't breathe." Arbery, Taylor, and Floyd were Black Americans. Black Lives Matter organized rallies across the United States. They wanted justice for these murders.

Hmong for Black Lives members participated in the rallies. Youa Vang Lee joined the George Floyd protests. Her son was Fong Lee. In 2006, 19-year-old Fong Lee was shot and killed by a police officer. The officer was found not guilty. Black American activists supported Lee's family. Lee said, "Here's what I saw with Fong: Black people were with us the whole time, morning or night . . . . We're very few. But, when we come together, we are many. We need to help them. And, they will help us when we need them."

In June 2020, hundreds marched in Chicago, Illinois. They marched from a Chinese American church to a Black American church. They supported Black Lives Matter. They wanted to build bridges between their communities.

Asian Americans faced racial unrest in 2020 as well. In December 2019, the COVID-19 pandemic began. President Donald Trump called COVID-19 the "Kung Flu" and the "China Virus." Such comments led to hate crimes against those with Asian backgrounds. Asian Americans were called racist names. They were harassed in the streets. They were attacked. Many elderly Asian Americans were targeted. On March 16, 2021, a man began shooting at a spa in Atlanta, Georgia. Six Asian American women were killed.

Black Lives Matter spoke out against attacks on Asian Americans. They said, "When we call for the eradication of White supremacy, we are saying that Asian Americans, and every other marginalized racial group, deserves to be freed from the violence, intimidation and fear . . . . None of us are free until we all are."

Many rallies and protests followed the Atlanta shootings. On March 21, 2021, there was a Black and Asian solidarity protest in New York City. People chanted, "Show me what community looks like. This is what community looks like!" A participant said, "The point is not one community versus another. The point is everybody versus racism."

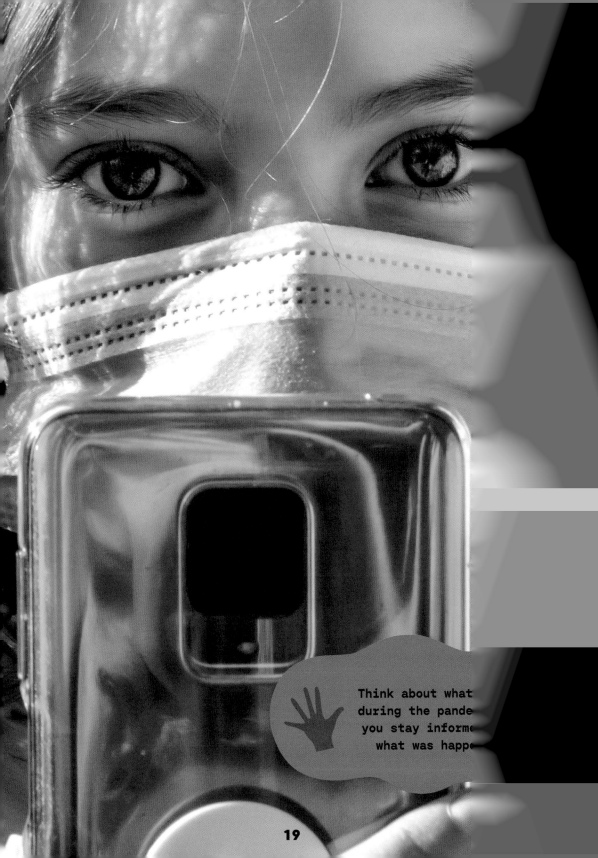

Think about what
during the pande
you stay informe
what was happe

CHAPTER 4

What Are Challenges to Building Asian-Black Solidarity?

As you have read, Asian-Black solidarity is alive and well. But it is not talked about as much as Asian-Black strife. Strife is angry or bitter disagreement. It is true that there have been and continue to be tensions between the two groups. Anti-Black racism exists in the Asian American community. Anti-Asian racism exists in the Black American community.

But such strife serves White supremacy. It doesn't serve liberation. Focusing on strife makes people of color compete with one another. It keeps communities of color from forming coalitions. These communities are too busy fighting each other to fight against White supremacy. White supremacy, which is the real root cause, wins in the end. It has created exclusion, segregation, and violence. Most of society's problems are caused by White supremacy. Asian and Black Americans are stronger together. People who support White supremacy know this. So they try to keep the groups apart.

Asian Americans have been called the "model minority." This is one of the major challenges preventing Asian-Black solidarity. It is a myth, or untrue story that many people believe. Asian Americans are viewed as being successful. So some White Americans set them up to be an example for other minority groups.

Think about examples of Asian-Black strife. How does this strife support White supremacy?

Think about the Model Minority Myth. How does this myth use Asian Americans as partners for White supremacy?

The Model Minority Myth is based on stereotypes. It assumes all Asian Americans are smart and hard-working. The myth is also based on colorism. Privileges are given to groups that are closer to Whiteness. It upholds Whiteness as the ideal. For example, data suggests Nigerian immigrants succeed more than Asian Americans. But Nigerians are seen as Black. Therefore, they are not models.

Having a "model minority" means there is a "problem minority." Specifically, the Model Minority Myth was created to diminish Black Americans. It developed during the 1960s, when Black Americans were fighting for civil rights. The myth was used as a racial wedge. It pitted Asian Americans against Black Americans. It blamed Black communities instead of racist laws. It says, "The system works. It's not the problem. See how well Asian Americans are doing. Why can't you be more like them? The problem must be you." Dr. Scott Kurashige is a university professor. He said, "The Model Minority stereotype really isn't meant to define Asian Americans. Rather, it's meant to define African Americans as deficient and inferior to White people by using Asian Americans as a proxy or a pawn to serve that purpose."

Early Asian immigrants wanted to assimilate. They wanted to fit in to avoid discrimination. They believed the Model Minority Myth. They also believed the myth of Black criminality. This myth is based on stereotypes. Black people are seen as criminals, poor, and uneducated. The media is flooded with images of Black people acting violent. For example, think about the Black Lives Matter protests. There were more images of looting and violence than of peaceful protests.

Most Black Americans are native-born Americans. They may be prone to xenophobia, which paints Asian Americans as "forever foreigners." White supremacy treats foreigners as scapegoats. It blames outsiders for many problems. Some Black communities may blame Asian Americans for their economic insecurity.

Asian and Black communities are both guilty of comparing oppression. They sometimes fight over who is more oppressed. They fight over who deserves more reparations. Instead they should be fighting against White supremacy.

Alicia Garza co-founded Black Lives Matter. She said, "We need to make sure that we're not falling into the wedges and the traps that get set for us. There is a long history of solidarity in Black communities and Asian communities—and those relationships are needed more than ever."

Think about the images you see in TV, movies, books, and other media. How are Asian and Black Americans portrayed?

BE IN THE KNOW!

Other concepts to know:

- **Cultural Humility** This is a commitment to learn about cultural differences. It is a commitment to address power imbalances between cultures.

- **Racial Binary** This is when people talk about racism in terms of Black and White people. It makes other people of color invisible.

CHAPTER 5

How Can We Be Better?

Now that you have learned about Asian-Black solidarity, let's work to support it.

We all come from different positions of privilege. We also have different types of privilege. Privilege is a special right or advantage. It is given to a chosen person or group. It is not earned. In the United States, being White is a privilege. Other examples include being male or an English speaker. It's hard to get ahead in a world that is not made for you. Use your privileges. Help oppressed people achieve equality.

Start with Yourself!

Everybody can do something. Just start somewhere. Start small. Build your self-awareness and your knowledge.

- Learn more about Asian-Black solidarity. Also, research other ways cultural groups have worked together. For example, Asian and Hispanic American communities have formed alliances many times.

- Learn more about anti-Blackness. Consider the role you play in supporting anti-Blackness. Consider how you benefit from anti-Blackness. Remember that no one truly benefits if harm is caused to anyone.

- Learn about community organizing. Learn from young people who have led movements.

- Unlearn the stereotypes you have about Asian and Black Americans. Consider how and why these stereotypes exist. Think about how they support White supremacy.

Think about your privileges. What powers and resources do you have?

Be an Ally!

Being an ally is the first step in racial justice work. Allies recognize their privilege. They use it in solidarity with others. They see something and they say something.

- Speak up when someone says that Asian and Black Americans hate each other. This is an incomplete story. Remind them of the many examples of Asian-Black solidarity. Discuss the role White supremacy plays in Asian-Black strife.

- Speak to friends and family members. Be willing to have hard and uncomfortable conversations. Educate others on the importance of Asian-Black solidarity.

- Speak with others from diverse racial groups. Understand each other's struggles.

Be an Accomplice!

Being an **accomplice** goes beyond allyship. Accomplices use their privilege. They challenge supremacy. They are willing to be uncomfortable. They stand up for equal rights.

- Stand with Asian and Black Americans. Volunteer for various organizations. Help raise funds and awareness.

- Stand for Asian and Black Americans. Create community safety plans. Work for police reform. Focus more on community services.

- Stand united against anti-Asian or anti-Black hate. Participate in peaceful protests and rallies. Make and carry solidarity signs. Be safe. Make sure an adult is with you.

Think about your powers and resources. How would your life be different without them?

Be an Activist!

Activists actively fight for political or social change. They give up their own privileges. They work together to fight against racism. They understand that if one group suffers, all groups suffer.

- Fight for Black Lives Matter. Support policies and practices that serve the most oppressed.

- Fight against the Model Minority Myth. Reject it. Soya Jung is an Asian American activist. Support her idea of a "Model Minority Mutiny." Do not allow one group to suffer while another group benefits.

- Fight to change laws and improve people's lives. Fight for living wages, fair housing, and food security. Remove the reasons for strife.

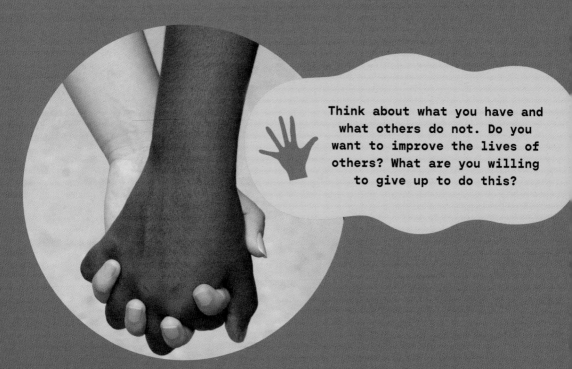

Think about what you have and what others do not. Do you want to improve the lives of others? What are you willing to give up to do this?

Take the Challenge!

Read all the books in the "Racial Justice in America" series. Engage in the community of activism. Create a podcast, newsletter, video, or social media campaign. Show up for the Asian American community. Include a segment about Asian-Black solidarity.

TASK: Interview Asian Americans and Black Americans. Interview people of different ages and backgrounds. Learn more about their experiences. Look for things they have in common. Look for ways they can work together.

Share your learning. Encourage others to learn more. Then, when you know more, do more. Commit to racial justice!

WHAT WOULD YOU DO?

Imagine your neighbor offers you a summer job. The neighbor says, "You can invite your Asian American friend to join you. But you can't invite your Black friend." How is this racist? How does this prevent Asian-Black solidarity? What would you do?

☐ Accept the job.   ☐ Refuse the job.

☐ Ask, "Are you kidding?"

EXTEND YOUR LEARNING

FICTION

Williams-Garcia, Rita. *One Crazy Summer*. New York, NY: Amistad, 2010.

NONFICTION

Loh-Hagan, Virginia. *A is for Asian American: An Asian Pacific Islander Desi American Alphabet Book*. Ann Arbor, MI: Sleeping Bear Press, 2022.

Nichols, Hedreich, and Kelisa Wing. *What is the Black Lives Matter Movement?* Ann Arbor, MI: Cherry Lake Publishing, 2021.

Public Broadcasting Service: Asian Americans
www.pbs.org/weta/asian-americans/

GLOSSARY

accomplice (uh-KAHM-pluhss) a person who uses their privilege to fight against supremacy

ally (AH-lye) a person who is aware of their privilege and supports oppressed communities

assimilate (uh-SIH-muh-layt) to fit in or be absorbed into the system

boycotts (BOI-kotss) bans or protests that involve refusing to buy something

colorism (KUH-luh-rih-zuhm) a system that discriminates against people with a dark skin tone

Desi (DEH-see) a word that describes people from India, Pakistan, or Bangladesh

enslaved (en-SLAYVD) someone forced to work without pay; enslaved people had no rights and could be bought and sold

ethnicities (eth-NIH-suh-teez) the states of belonging to a social group that has a common national or cultural tradition

inclusive (ihn-KLOO-siv) allowing all kinds of people to belong

myth (MITH) a story that is not true but is widely believed

privileges (PRIV-lih-jez) unearned rights or advantages given to a chosen person or group

racial wedge (RAY-shuhl WEJ) a group used to split apart communities of color in an attempt to decrease the strength of a group

reparations (reh-puh-RAY-shuhnz) the making of amends for a wrong one has done by paying money to or otherwise helping those who have been wronged

scapegoats (SKAYP-gohtss) people or groups being blamed

solidarity (sah-luh-DEHR-uh-tee) a political union or strategy where people join forces to fight for a common goal

stereotypes (STEHR-ee-uh-typess) widely held ideas or beliefs many people have about a thing or group, which may be untrue or only partly true

strife (STRYF) angry or bitter disagreement

supremacy (suh-PREH-muh-see) the idea that one group is superior to other groups and thus is given privileges to maintain that power

xenophobia (zeh-nuh-FOH-bee-uh) the fear or dislike of people from other countries

INDEX